# Contemporary Aural Course

## set eight
## 'hear more chords!'

### by Margaret Brandman

Exclusive distributors for Australian and New Zealand
Encore Music Distributors
6 Abbott St, Alphington
Victoria 3078 Australia
This book © Copyright 2024 Jazzem Music
46 Gerrale St, Cronulla, NSW 2230, Australia
ISBN 978-0-949683-31-1
Book MMP 8029
Audio MMP 8030
Book and Audio pack MMP 8031

# CONTEMPORARY AURAL COURSE

## set eight
## 'hear more chords!'

# INTRODUCTION

Welcome to another advancing level of the Contemporary Aural Course, Set Eight: 'Hear More Chords!'

These courses are designed to assist students to progress further in the Popular and Jazz fields, as well as understand and recognise the sounds heard in Classical Music. This set continues the topic of the sounds and functions of modern chords along with the modes or scales that can be sounded together with them. The new material begins in Lesson Two with the Minor 6th chord followed by Half Diminished 7th chord in Lesson Three.

There is also a section devoted to frequently used Chromatic chords found in classical music, and the progression from these sounds to the substitute chords used in Jazz.

When new chords are introduced, they will be sounded in a sequence which allows the listener to sing along with the repeated playing of the Broken forms of the chord. Students should be encouraged to develop their vocal abilities. Their own voices will become 'portable instruments' and a reliable means of reproducing the pitches heard, so that music played on instruments of different timbre can be converted to their own familiar vocal sounds.

For written practice and practical examples of the topics presented in this set, refer to the Contemporary Theory Workbook, Books 1 and 2, Contemporary Chord Workbook, Book 1, and Books 2 to 4 of the Contemporary Piano Method all by Margaret Brandman. The set of pieces 'Dreamweaving' demonstrates all the standard four-note chords, including the minor 6th and half-diminished seventh chords.

This course is written and presented by Margaret Brandman. Special thanks to Ross Hutchison for the introduction on the CD and to Ian Robertson for his work on the recording.

Refer to the website: **www.margaretbrandman.com** for more information on supporting publications.

**Margaret Brandman (Dr)**
Ph.D (Mus/Arts), B. Mus.(Comp), T.Mus.A
F.Comp. ASMC., F.Mus.Ed.ASMC., L.Perf. ASMC
Hon.FNMSM., A.Mus.A., ASA T.Dip.
International Woman of the Year for
services to music 2003 (IBC)

# CONTENTS

*ANSWER SHEET INCLUDED   Key:  T.N.  -  Track Number*

# LESSON ONE

Track No.

#2

| CHORD TYPES | MATCHING MODES |
|---|---|

### Major Seventh Chord — Ionian or Lydian Mode

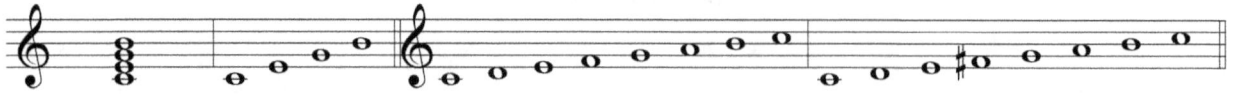

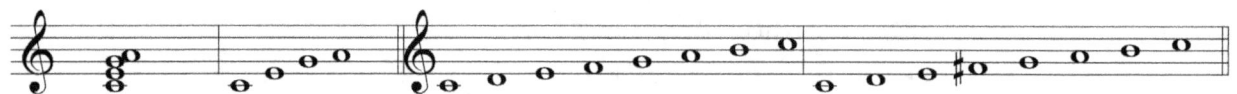

### Dominant Seventh Chord — Mixolydian Mode

### Diminished Seventh Chord — Diminished Scale

### Major Sixth Chord — Ionian or Lydian Mode

### Minor Seventh Chord — Dorian Mode

| Chord Types | Chord Symbols |
|---|---|
| Major 7th | maj7, ma7 or △ |
| Dominant 7th | 7 |
| Diminished 7th | o7 |
| Major 6th | 6 |
| Minor 7th | mi7 or -7 |

# LESSON ONE

Track No.

**#3** | **Question 1.**

ANSWERS    (1)..............    (2)..............    (3)..............    (4)..............    (5)..............

**#4** | **Question 2.**

ANSWERS    (1)..............    (2)..............    (3)..............    (4)..............    (5)..............

**#5-8** | **Listening Section:** Scales and Modes

**#9-10** | **Question 3.**

|  | Chord | Mode | Chord | Mode | Chord | Mode |
|---|---|---|---|---|---|---|
| ANSWERS (1) | .........., | .............| | .............., | .............| | .............., | .............| |
| (2) | .........., | .............| | .............., | .............| | .............., | .............| |

**#11-12** | **Question 4.**    FRERE JACQUES

Identify the chord qualities. Letter names are not required.

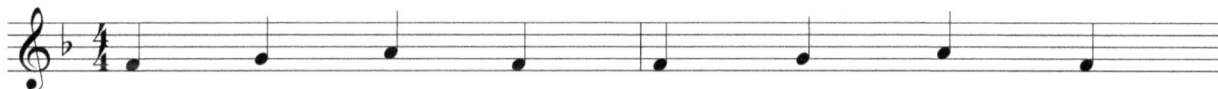

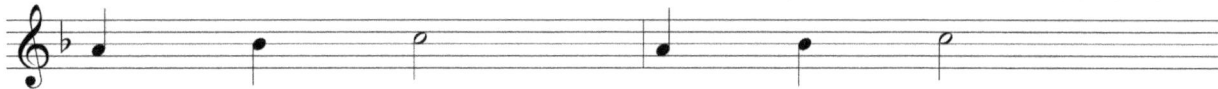

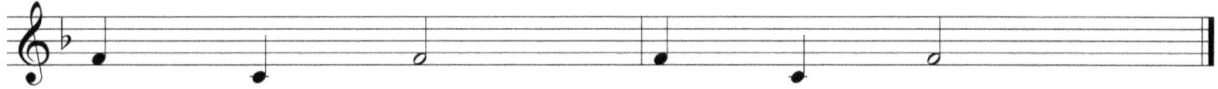

Track No.

# LESSON TWO

## THE MINOR SIXTH CHORD

#13

Cmi6   compare to:   C6        Compare:  Cmi6   -   Cmi7

mi triad & Maj 6th interval     Maj triad & Maj 6th interval          mi triad & mi7 interval

#14

*Dorian Mode           mi 6th       *asc. Melodic Minor scale       mi 6th

*Refer to:  Contemporary Chord Workbook 1 - pp46 & 47*

#15

## Chord Progressions

#16-17

### Question 1.

e.g.    Chord symbol for G Major 6th = G6
        Chord symbol for E minor 6th = Emi6

The letter names are given.  Write 6 or mi6 next to each letter name, according to the sounds played on the audio.

ANSWERS        (1). E.........    (2). A.........    (3). E♭.........    (4). B♭.........

#18-19

### Question 2.

ANSWERS        (1). G.........    (2). B.........    (3). D.........    (4). F.........

#20-21

### Question 3.

Chord choices:

Rest chords - beginning, middle or end:
        *Major 7th, Major 6th, Minor 6th, Maj Triad, Minor Triad*
Leading Function chords - second to last chords:
        *Dominant 7th, Diminished 7th*
Secondary Leading Function chords - chords two and/or three:
        *Minor 7th, Minor 6th*

ANSWERS        (1)........., ............., ............., ............., .............

        (2)........., ............., ............., .............

        (3)........., ............., ............., .............

        (4)........., ............., ............., ............., .............

# LESSON THREE

## THE HALF DIMINISHED SEVENTH OR
## MINOR SEVENTH FLATTENED FIFTH CHORD

Track No.

**#22**

C mi6th  -  Root Pos  1st inv  2nd inv  3rd inv

**#23-24**

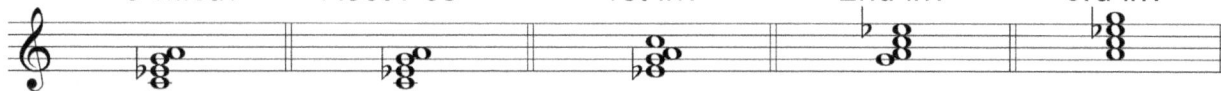

Half Diminished 7th ⌀  Construction

C ⌀

dim triad  &  mi 7th interval

Compare
Half Diminished 7th  to Full Diminished 7th

C ⌀  C°7

dim triad & dim 7th interval

**#25**

ALTERNATIVE NAME
⌀ = Minor 7th Flattened 5th - mi7♭5  :  Locrian Mode

Progressions using the half dim 7th

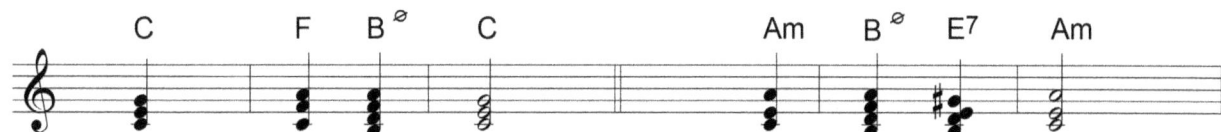

C  F  B⌀  C  Am  B⌀  E7  Am

1) Key: C  I  IV  vii⌀  I  2) Key: Ami  i  ii⌀-  V7  i

*Refer to:  Contemporary Chord Workbook 1 - pp48 & 49*

**8.**

# LESSON THREE - continued

## Question 1.

Write the chord symbols above each chord and notate the chord in full above the given notes. Then write the degree numbers below each chord, using upper case roman numerals for any chord with a major triad at the base, and lower case roman numerals for those chords with minor or diminished triads at the base of the chord. eg. V or iii

Symbols:

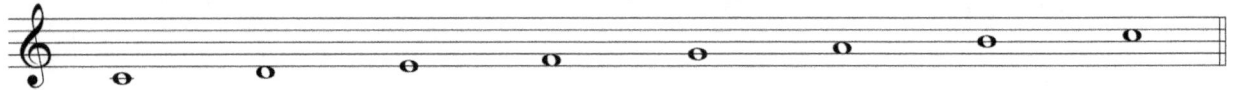

Degrees:

a) What types of 7th chords occur on the First and Fourth degrees of the major scale? ..........................

b) What types of 7th chords occur on Second, Third and Sixth degrees of the major scale?....................

c) What type of 7th chord occurs on the Fifth degree of the major scale? ...............................................

**Listening Section:** Refer to previous page

## Question 2.

ANSWERS  (1).............     (2)..............     (3)..............     (4)..............

## Question 3.

Chord Choices:
Major 6th, Minor 6th, Minor 7th, Half Diminished 7th

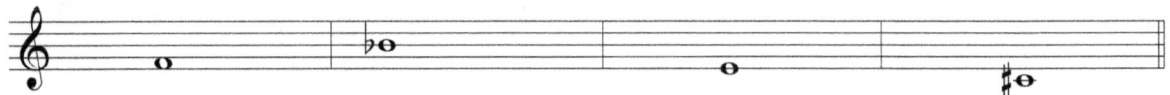

ANSWERS (1).............     (2)..............     (3)..............     (4)..............

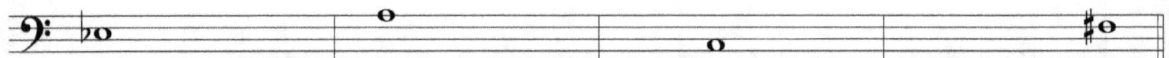

(5).............     (6)...............     (7)..............     (8)..............

# LESSON THREE - continued

**#36-37** **Question 4.**

| | Chord | Mode | Chord | Mode |
|---|---|---|---|---|
| ANSWERS | (1)............., | ...................| | (2)............., | ...................| |
| | (3)............., | ...................| | (4)............., | ...................| |

**#38** **LISTENING**

Chord Sequence
Major 7th, Dominant 7th, Minor 7th, Minor 7th flat 5 = Half-Diminished 7th, Diminished 7th, Minor 6th, Major 6th

**#39-40** **Question 5.**

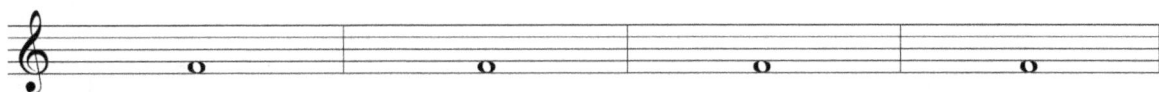

ANSWERS  (1)..............    (2)..............    (3)..............    (4)..............

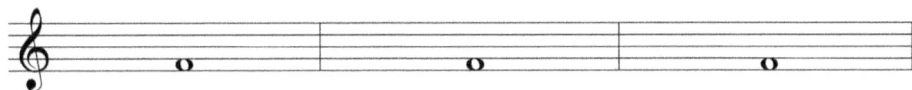

(5)..............    (6)..............    (7)..............

**#41** **Question 6.**

Chord choices:

| **First Chord** | **Second Chord** | **Third Chord** | **Final Chord** |
|---|---|---|---|
| maj or min | secondary leading | leading function | rest chord |
| M6 or m6 | | | |

**Rest chords - beginning, middle or end:**
   Major 7th, Major 6th, Minor 6th, Maj triad, Minor triad
**Leading Function chords:**
   Dominant 7th, Diminished 7th
**Secondary Leading tendency chords:**
   Minor 7th, Minor 6th

**#42**        ANSWERS        (1)........., ............., ............., .............

(2)........., ............., ............., .............

(3)........., ............., ............., .............

(4)........., ............., ............., .............

# LESSON THREE - continued

**Question 7.**

## God Rest Ye Merry Gentlemen

Track No.

# LESSON FOUR - Part A
## CHROMATIC CHORDS FOUND IN CLASSICAL HARMONY

CD-2:
#1

Neapolitan 6th | Italian 6th | German 6th | Dom 7th

Key: C    ♭II        ♭VI        ♭VI *        Sounds like *

*Refer to Contemporary Piano Method Book 3, for detailed information.*

## Resolutions of the Neapolitan 6th

#2

I    ♭II⁶    V7    I        I    ♭II⁶    I⁶₄    V    I

* Bass note is doubled
to create a four note chord

#3    *Excerpt from Beethoven's Moonlight Sonata*

## Resolutions of the German 6th

#4-5

I    IV    I    ♭VI    V    I        I    ♭VI    *I⁶₄    V    I

* Second Inversion - Bass note
is still V

#6    *Excerpt from Mozarts Sonata in F K332*
*German 6th, and Italian 6th*

#7-8

## Question 1.
Indicate Chromatic chords:   ♭VI -g 6th.,   ♭II np

eg.   I / maj ,   ♭II / MAJ ,   ♭VI / Gm6 ,   I / MAJ

ANSWERS   (1)......... / ......... ,   ......... / ......... ,   ......... / ......... ,   ......... / ......... ,   ......... / .........

(2)......... / ......... ,   ......... / ......... ,   ......... / ......... ,   ......... / .........

(3)......... / ......... ,   ......... / ......... ,   ......... / ......... ,   ......... / .........

(4)......... / ......... ,   ......... / ......... ,   ......... / ......... ,   ......... / .........

12.

Track No.
#9

# LESSON FOUR - Part B

## ALTERED DOMINANT 7ths and the FRENCH 6th

*Refer to CPM Bk 3, p26 before commencing this section*

#10-13  1) Dominant 7th♯5th        Third inversion Dom 7th♯5
Symbols: 7♯5 or 7+       resolved to Major Triad

C Aug triad  +  m7th  =  C7♯5      Preferred Inversion:  C7♯5  -  F

---

#14-15  2) Dominant 7th♭5        C7♭5 becomes G♭7♭5

C7♭5

R   1   2   3   R

R   1   2   3   R

G♭7♭5

( ↕ - indicates same chord)

---

Progression using Dom 7th         Progression using Dominant 7th♭5         Same progression root notes moving by semitones

Dm7  G7  C        Dm7  G7♭5  C        Dm7  D♭7♭5  C

#16-17

ii  Ⅴ7  I        ii  *Ⅴ7♭5  I        ii  *♭Ⅱ  I

* Refer to p27 CPM Bk 3        French 6th used on ♭Ⅱ

---

## The French 6th  Progressions

Fr 6th        OR        Fr 6th

#18-19

dim 5th

I  Ⅳ  I  ♭Ⅵ  Ⅴ  I        I  ♭Ⅵ  *I⁶₄  Ⅴ  I
       **

** NB. Some composers spell this chord 1, 3, ♯4, ♯6  (instead of ♭5)

#20  **LISTENING:** Compare Italian, German and French 6ths.

# LESSON FOUR - Continued

**#21-23** | **Listening Section:** Mozart Sonata in Am K.310 Excerpt: French 6th

**#24** | Chopin Prelude Op 28 No. 20: altered 7ths

**#25** | COMPARE SEVENTHS

**#26-27** | **Question 2.**

Choices: 7, 7♯5, 7♭5

ANSWERS  (1)............ (2)............ (3)............ (4)............ (5)............ (6)............

**#28-29** | **Question 3.** Choices:   Maj7,   Maj6 ‖  Dom7,   Dom7♭5,   Dom7♯5,
Min7,   Min6 ‖
°7,   ∅7   ‖

ANSWERS  (1).............. (2).............. (3).............. (4)..............

(5).............. (6).............. (7).............. (8).............. (9)..............

**#30-31** | **Question 4.**

Symbols:

Degrees:   (1)........., ..........., ..........., ...........   (2)........., ..........., ..........., ..........

Symbols:

Degrees:   (3)........, ..........., ..........., ...........   (4)........, ..........., ..........., ..........

**#32-33** | **Question 5.   Chromatic Progressions**

Chord type and degree - e.g.  ♭VI   -   Fr 6th

ANSWERS  (1).......... - .........., | .......... - .........., | .......... - .........., .......... - .........., | .......... - .......... ‖

(2).......... - .........., | .......... - .........., .......... - .........., | .......... - .......... ‖

(3).......... - .........., | .......... - .........., .......... - .........., | .......... - .......... ‖

**14.**

# LESSON FIVE
## MORE ALTERED SEVENTHS

**#34-37** | **PART A**

Major 7th      Major 7th♯5      Major 7th♭5      D9$^{(13)}$

**#38-39** | **Question 1.**

ANSWERS    (1)............ (2)............ (3)............ (4)............ (5)............ (6)............

**#40-41** | **Question 2.**

ANSWERS    (1)............ (2)............ (3)............ (4)............ (5)............ (6)............

---

**#42** | **PART B**

**1)** **The minor (major 7th) chord**
**aka: minor sharpened 7th chord**

Cmi

**Harmonic Minor Scale**                mi♯7 or mi(maj7th)

**#43** | **Progressions**

Am    B$^{ø}$    E7    Am(maj7)    Emi    Emi♯7    Emi7    Emi6

i    ii$^{ø}$    V7    i♯7

Track No.

**#44**

## 2) The Dominant 7th Suspended 4th - symbol (7sus4)

C7sus4   or   C7sus

Csus4

mi7th

+   =

Resolution

C7sus4   C7   F

List all of the altered 7ths heard in Lessons Four and Five

Dom7♯5     Dom7♭5     Maj7♯5     Maj7♭5     Mi(maj7)     Dom7sus4

---

**#45-46**

### Question 3.

ANSWERS    (1)............ (2)............ (3)............ (4)............

**#47**

### Question 4.

ANSWERS    (1)............ (2)............ (3)............ (4)............ (5)............ (6)............

**#48-49**

### Question 5.

ANSWERS (1)............    (2)............    (3)............    (4)............    (5)............    (6)............

**#50**

### Question 6.    Excerpts from Bach's Prelude No. 12 in F minor.

**#52-53**

Part 1:    .............,    .............,    .............,    .............,    .............

**#54-55**

Part 2:    .............,    .............,    .............

**#56-57**

Part 3:    ...........................................

**16.**

# LESSON SIX
## REVIEW

**Question 1.**

ANSWERS    (1)............ (2)............ (3)............ (4)............ (5)............

**Question 2.**

|  | Chord | Mode | Chord | Mode |
|---|---|---|---|---|

ANSWERS    (1)................, ...................    (2)................, ...................

(3)................, ...................    (4)................, ...................

(5)................, ...................    (6)................, ...................

(7)................, ...................

**Question 3.**

ANSWERS    (1)............ (2)............ (3)............ (4)............ (5)............ (6)............

**Question 4.**

Chord choices:  mi, maj, maj7, 7, mi7, ⌀ , ○7, mi6, 6,
                7♯5, 7♭5, Maj7♯5, Maj7♭5,  mi♯7, 7sus

(1) .............,    .............,    .............

(2) .............,    .............,    .............

(3) .............,    .............,    .............

(4) .............,    .............,    .............

Track No.

#64

## Question 5.

ANSWERS☐　　(1) ............,☐　............,☐　............

(2) ............,☐　............,☐　............

(3) ............,☐　............,☐　............

(4) ............,☐　............,☐　............

#65-66

## Question 6.　　Colours

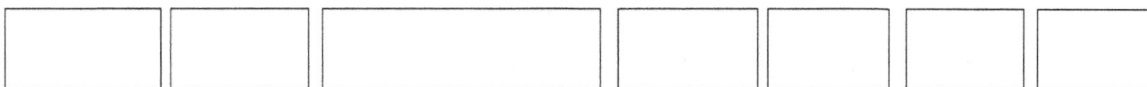

# Contemporary Aural Course
set eight

# ANSWER SHEETS

## ANSWER SHEET — LESSON TWO

**Question 1.**
ANSWERS  (1) ..... m6   (2) ..... 6   (3) ..... 6   (4) ..... m6

**Question 2.**
ANSWERS  (1) ..... m7   (2) ..... m6   (3) ..... m6   (4) ..... m7

**Question 3.**
ANSWERS
(1) I / Maj   ii / m7   IV / 6   vii / °7   I / Maj
(2) i / m6   iv / m6   ii / m7   i / m6
(3) I / 6   ii / m7   V / 7   V / 7   vi / mi
(4) I / maj7   vi / mi7   ii / m7   V / 7   I / 6

## LESSON THREE

**Question 1.**
Symbols: Cmaj7  Dm7  Em7  Fmaj7  G7  Am7  B∅  Cmaj7
Degrees:  I    ii    iii   IV    V    vi   vii   VIII

**Question 2.**
ANSWERS  (1) ..... ∅   (2) ..... m6   (3) ..... ∅   (4) ..... m6

**Question 3.**
ANSWERS  (1) ..... m7   (2) ..... 6   (3) ..... m6   (4) ..... m6
(5) ..... 6   (6) ..... ∅   (7) ..... m6   (8) ..... m7

## ANSWER SHEET — LESSON ONE

**Question 1.**
ANSWERS  (1) ..... 6   (2) ..... °7   (3) ..... m7   (4) ..... 7   (5) ..... maj7

**Question 2.**
ANSWERS  (1) ..... m7   (2) ..... 7   (3) ..... 6   (4) ..... maj7   (5) ..... °7

**Question 3.**

| | Chord | Mode | Chord | Mode | Chord | Mode |
|---|---|---|---|---|---|---|
| ANSWERS (1) | m7 | Dorian | 7 | Mixolydian | 6 | Lydian |
| (2) | 6 | Ionian | °7 | Diminished Scale | maj7 | Lydian |

**Question 4.  FRERE JACQUES**

# ANSWER SHEET
## LESSON THREE Continued

**Question 7.**

God Rest Ye Merry Gentlemen

---

# ANSWER SHEET
## LESSON THREE Continued

**Question 4.**

ANSWERS

| | Chord | Mode | | Chord | Mode |
|---|---|---|---|---|---|
| (1) | m6 | Dorian | (2) | 6 | Lydian |
| (3) | m7 | Dorian | (4) | ⌀ | Locrian |

**Question 5.**

ANSWERS
- (1) ○7
- (2) 6
- (3) m7
- (4) maj7
- (5) ⌀
- (6) 7
- (7) m6

**Question 6.**

ANSWERS
- (1) I / Maj, ii / m7, Ⅴ / 7, I / Maj7
- (2) i / mi, iv / m7, vii / ○7, i / m6
- (3) I / 6, vi / m7, vii / ⌀, I / 6
- (4) i / Maj, ii / ⌀, Ⅴ / 7, i / m6

# ANSWER SHEET
## LESSON FIVE

**Question 1.**
ANSWERS  (1) maj7#5  (2) maj7  (3) maj7♭5  (4) maj7  (5) maj7♭5  (6) maj7#5

**Question 2.**
ANSWERS  (1) 7♭5  (2) 7#5  (3) maj7  (4) 7#5  (5) 7  (6) maj7♭5

**Question 3.**  NB: mi#7 = mi(maj7)

**Question 4.**
ANSWERS  (1) 7sus  (2) mi#7  (3) mi#7  (4) 7sus  (5) mi#7  (6) maj7♭5

**Question 4.**
ANSWERS  (1) 7#5  (2) 7sus  (3) maj7#5  (4) 7♭5  (5) mi#7  (6) maj7♭5

**Question 5.**
ANSWERS (1) 7sus  (2) 7♭5  (3) maj7#5  (4) mi#7  (5) maj7♭5  (6) 7#5

**Question 6.**

Part 1:  ø  ...  mi  ...  7♭5  ...  maj

Part 2:  ...  7  ...  7  ...  mi#7

Part 3:  ...  German 6th


# ANSWER SHEET
## LESSON FOUR

**Question 1.**
ANSWERS
(1) I / Maj , ♭VI / Gmn6 , I⁶₄ / Maj , V7 / 7 , I / Maj
(2) i / mi , ♭II / Np , V7 / 7 , i / mi ,
(3) I / Maj , ♭II / Np , I⁶₄ / Maj , V / Maj , I / Maj
(4) i / mi , ♭VI / Gmn6 , V7 / 7 , i / mi

**Question 2.**
ANSWERS  (1) G7♭5  (2) B7  (3) D♭7#5  (4) E7  (5) C7♭5  (6) A♭7#5

**Question 3.**
ANSWERS  (1) m7  (2) 7♭5  (3) 6  (4) °7
(5) maj7  (6) 7#5  (7) m6  (8) 7  (9) ø

**Question 4.**

**Question 5.**
ANSWERS
(1) I – maj , ♭VI – Fr6th , I⁶₄ – maj , V7 – 7 , I – maj ‖
(2) I – maj , ♭II⁶₃ – Np , V7 – 7 , I – maj ‖
(3) i – mi , ♭VI – Gmn6th , V7 – 7 , i – mi ‖

# ANSWER SHEET
# LESSON SIX
# REVIEW

**Question 1.**

ANSWERS (1) mi (2) Aug (3) sus4 (4) maj (5) dim

**Question 2.**

ANSWERS

| Chord | Mode | | Chord | Mode |
|-------|------|--|-------|------|
| (1) 7 | Mixolydian | | (2) ⌀ | Locrian |
| (3) maj7 | Lydian | | (4) m7 | Dorian |
| (5) 6 | Major | | (6) °7 | Diminished |
| (7) m6 | Dorian | | | |

**Question 3.**

ANSWERS (1) maj7#5 (2) mi#7 (3) 7sus4 (4) maj7b5 (5) 7#5 (6) 7b5

**Question 4.**

(1) m7 ........ 7 ........ maj7#5

(2) ⌀ ........ 7b5 ........ mi

(3) mi#7 ........ m7 ........ m6

(4) 7 ........ 7#5 ........ 6

# ANSWER SHEET
# LESSON SIX Continued
# REVIEW

**Question 5.**

ANSWERS (1) maj7 ........ ⌀ ........ 6

(2) ........ 7b5 ........ 7 ........ maj7

(3) °7 ........ 7sus ........ mi#7

(4) 6 ........ °7 ........ maj7

**Question 6.   Colours**